My Daily
DELIGHT
IN THE
LORD

BY

DR. MARILYN NEUBAUER

Marilyn Neubauer Ministries
P.O. Box 4664
Oceanside, CA 92052

(760) 439-1401

www.marilynneubauer.com

Published by Marilyn Neubauer Ministries
P.O. Box 4664
Oceanside, CA 92052

Cover design by Wilson Design & Publishing

Table of Contents

Introduction 1

Chapter 1 7
Delighting Daily in the Lord

Chapter 2 14
Created to Worship

Chapter 3 15
Pure in His Presence

Chapter 4 16
Enter into His Courts with Praise

Chapter 5 18
Boldly Proclaim Faith's Confessions

Chapter 6 20
An Ambassador for Christ

Chapter 7 22
Financial Blessings

Chapter 8 23
Victory for Family, Leaders and Nations

Chapter 9 24
God's Medicine for Healing and Staying Healthy

Chapter 10 25
Our Covenant Keeping God

Personal Thoughts, Prayers and Victories 26

Introduction

We were created to worship our Heavenly Father. This prayer book takes us into a place of worship before praying and before making our confessions of faith. As we acknowledge who He is and exalt Him, it ushers in His presence. In His presence we find joy and peace. His joy becomes our strength. As we turn our focus on Him in His presence, our confidence rises and we proclaim our confessions of faith with boldness.

The word *confession* means to say the same as or to speak in parallel with. When we confess God's Word that means we say what He says. Our mouth and heart are in agreement with Him. God's Word then becomes alive and powerful, causing dynamic results.

The Bible tells us that we, as the saints of God, overcome by the blood of the Lamb and the word of our testimony (Revelation 12:11). As our confessions are reinforced with His Word, then we know we are in agreement with what the Bible declares about our situation and we can expect to overcome. The Lord watches over His Word to perform it (Jeremiah 1:12) and His Word does not return void (Isaiah 55:11). As we speak His Word then we have the assurance that that is what He will bring to pass.

We read in Romans 8:29 we are to be conformed into the image of Christ Jesus. We also read in John 12:49 Jesus only spoke what the Father told Him to speak. Therefore, if we are to be conformed into the image of Jesus, then we too are to speak what the Father tells us to speak. Life and death are in the power of the tongue (Proverbs 18:21). The words we speak have the power to bring life or death, victory or defeat. If we speak what the Bible says, then we are being conformed into the image of Jesus and we will overcome the daily attacks of the evil one.

As we proclaim faith's confessions for our personal life, our loved ones, friends, co-workers and ministry, we can expect the Word of God to work mightily. Jesus said He came to give us abundant life (John 10:10). As we proclaim the Word of God in our daily lives, we will begin to walk in this triumphant life He has provided for us (2 Corinthians 2:14).

I pray this prayer book will greatly enhance your prayer life.

June 22, 2007

Ms. Marilyn Neubauer
Post Office Box 4664
Oceanside, California 92052-4664

Dear Ms. Neubauer,

Thank you for your kind letter and for the copy of *My Daily Delight in the Lord*. President Bush and I are grateful for your words of support and your prayers.

President Bush and I are sustained by our faith and find that a strong faith makes everything about life easier. We are touched and uplifted by the knowledge that so many across America are praying for us.

The President joins me in sending best wishes.

Sincerely,

Laura Bush

My Daily DELIGHT IN THE LORD

*Delight yourself also in the LORD
and He will give you the desires
of your heart.*

Psalm 37:4 (NKJV)

*For in my inner being I delight
in God's law.*

Romans 7:22 (NIV)

5

Chapter 1
Delighting Daily in the Lord

As believers we are called to delight in Him.

Delight yourself also in the Lord, and He will give you the desires of your heart. Psalm 37:4

To delight in someone is to take great pleasure in being in his or her presence.

It is a joy to Jesus when a person takes time to walk more intimately with Him. – Oswald Chambers

When we come to the place of delighting in the Lord, we will come to the place of intimacy, the secret place. It is a place where the child of God can live that the world doesn't even know exists.

What a privilege it is that the Lord has invited us to dwell in His presence, a place of safety where we can learn to trust Him totally.

He who dwells in the secret place of the Most High shall abide under the shadow of the Almighty. I will say of the LORD, "He is my refuge and my fortress; My God, in Him I will trust." Psalm 91:1-2

The word *dwell* represents the place where one abides, where one delights in being.

Setting A Priority

To delight in the Lord is a choice we make daily. It must be or become a priority in our lives. The following scriptures from the Old Testament are examples of those who often set a priority of rising early to be with the Lord.

Abraham rose early to go to the mount where the Lord commanded him to go (Genesis 22:3). **Moses rose early** to go up Mt. Sinai as the Lord commanded him to do (Exodus 34:4). **Joshua rose early** in the morning as the Lord commanded them to walk around the city (Joshua 6:12). **Samuel's parents rose early** to worship the Lord (1 Samuel 1:19).

There is an effort involved in setting time aside to be with the Lord. One must make it a priority. Jesus had such a priority:

And when He had sent the multitudes away, He went up on the mountain by Himself to pray.   Matthew 14:23

And it happened, as He was alone praying, that His disciples joined Him.   Luke 9:18

And in the morning, rising up a great while before day, He went out, and departed into a solitary place, and there prayed.   Mark 1:35

Jesus rose a great while before daybreak. Perhaps it was 4 or 5 in the morning. Prayer was a priority with Jesus. He received strength and peace in the secret place.

We are all invited to come to a solitary place to worship and have daily fellowship with Him.

Developing Intimacy With The Lord

Developing intimacy with the Lord begins with setting a priority to delight daily in Him. Worship is the highest form of prayer. Worship means to draw close with the

8

intent to kiss. As we make it a priority to worship Him through prayer and fellowship in His presence, we begin to cultivate a relationship of intimacy.

But the hour is coming, and now is, when the true worshippers will worship the Father in spirit and truth; for the Father is seeking such to worship Him. John 4:23

The word *intimacy* expresses a deep love for someone.

We sense the heart cry from the Apostle Paul whom God used to write over two-thirds of the New Testament, when he penned these words:

For my determined purpose is that I may know Him that I may <u>progressively</u> become more deeply and <u>intimately acquainted with Him</u>, perceiving and recognizing and understanding the wonders of His Person more strongly and more clearly, and that I may in that same way come to know the power outflowing from His resurrection.
Philippians 3:10a AMP

Knowing Him intimately does not happen overnight, it must be cultivated through time spent with Him.

Intimacy not only means to love deeply but it also means to trust without any reservations.

*Trust in the LORD with **<u>all your heart</u>**, and lean not on your own understanding.* Proverbs 3:5

*Jesus said to him: you shall love the LORD your God with **<u>all your heart</u>**, with all your soul, and with all your mind. This is the first and great commandment. And the second is like it: You shall love your neighbor as yourself.*
Matthew 22:37-38

Paul once again expresses the depth of his love and sincere gratitude in knowing Christ.

I consider everything a loss compared to the surpassing greatness of knowing Christ Jesus my Lord, for whose sake I have lost all things.   Philippians 3:8

Through Intimacy We Receive Impartation

As we fellowship with the Lord in prayer, we must learn to be still and listen for He has much to impart.

It was of upmost importance to Jesus that all would know His love and commitment to obeying His Father's instructions no matter the cost. It was during His intimate times of prayer that He received instructions as to His divine assignment and His strength to follow through with this assignment.

But that the world may know that I love the Father, and as the Father gave Me commandment, so I do.   John 14:31

I do as the Father has commanded Me, so that the world may know (be convinced) that I love the Father and that I do only what the Father has instructed Me to do. (I act in full agreement with His orders.)   John 14:31 AMP

Just as the Father imparted instructions, guidance, and strength to Jesus, so it is with us.

However, when He, the Spirit of truth, has come, He will guide you into all truth; for He will not speak on His own authority, but whatever He hears He will speak; and He will tell you things to come.   John 16:13

The Holy Spirit hears from the Father and tells us what He

hears, guiding us to only do what the Father has instructed us to do, just as He did with Jesus. These times of intimacy with the Father will keep us in a safe place and in alignment with His divine assignment for our lives.

Intimacy Can Be Blocked

We cannot be intimate with the Lord or anyone else if there is a lack of trust and uncertainty of being loved.

We are to trust in the Lord with all our heart and without any reservations. A heart filled with worry and anxiety is a heart that isn't trusting in the Lord. This is a heart going in the wrong direction. It has more faith in the devil to steal, kill, and destroy than in God to provide protection and to perform His Word.

Other times we may be fearful or even doubt that God's Word will work for us even though we acknowledge it is true. Often thoughts like this come from a lack of knowing His love. The Bible tells us that we are to be rooted and grounded in love (Ephesians 3:16-19). When you truly know He loves you, walking by faith comes so much easier.

According to Mark 11:22 we are to have faith in God, have childlike faith, and simply believe.

I remember in Sunday school we sang a song that went like this: *Jesus loves me this I know, for the Bible tells me so.* How simple this should be to understand.

But without faith it is impossible to please Him, for he who comes to God must believe that He is, and that He is a rewarder of those who diligently seek Him. Hebrews 11:6

Just as we can physically have clogged arteries in our heart, worry can cause clogged arteries in our spiritual heart stopping the heart from pumping faith. Then our confessions become merely words having no life in them at all.

Confessions of faith must come from our spirit, a spiritual heart filled with faith, love and trust. When our spirit is overflowing with faith, love, and trust in God, the words we speak become life and they bring us to a place of victory.

Removing Blockages

To remove blockages we must make the decision today to trust in the Lord with **all** our hearts and to meditate on His Word day and night (Psalm 1:1-3).

I will say of the Lord, He is my refuge and my fortress, my God; in Him will I trust.   Psalm 91:2

Give Him dominion over your thinking. Take negative thoughts captive (2 Corinthians 10:5). Don't feed on those thoughts that cause worry, fear or anxiety. Let us unclog the arteries of our spiritual hearts, and only believe.

Finally, brethren, whatsoever things are true, whatsoever things are honest, whatsoever things are just, whatsoever things are pure, whatsoever things are lovely, whatsoever things are of good report; if there be any virtue, and if there be any praise, think on these things. Those things, which ye have both learned, and received, and heard, and seen in me, do: and the God of peace shall be with you.
                                          Philippians 4:8-9

Another old favorite hymn of mine is: *What a Friend We Have in Jesus.* The words of this hymn remind me that

Jesus truly is my friend and that He cares about every area and detail of my life.

This song encourages my heart to not be worried or anxious about anything.

> *What a friend we have in Jesus,*
> *All our sins and griefs to bear!*
> *What a privilege to carry,*
> *Everything to God in prayer.*
> *Oh, what peace we often forfeit,*
> *Oh, what needless pain we bear,*
> *All because we do not carry,*
> *Everything to God in prayer.*

Casting all your cares upon Him; for he careth for you.

1 Peter 5:7

Often times it seems easier to say than do. This is when we ask the Lord for His grace and strength to get us to the place of complete trust in Him. He yearns for intimacy with each of us and is ever present to help us get to this place.

O, the fullness, the pleasure, the sheer excitement of knowing God here on earth. — Jim Elliott

Begin to cultivate a relationship of intimacy with the Lord. Make it a priority to delight in Him daily. Once we come to the place of complete trust in Him, we are now able to declare our confessions of faith and they will be life to every situation we encounter.

Chapter 2
Created to Worship

We were created to delight in the Lord daily, to worship and commune with our Creator. The avenue to intimacy with our Father comes through thanksgiving and praise.

Enter into His gates with thanksgiving,
And into His courts with praise.
Be thankful to Him, and bless His name.
Psalm 100:4

The Lord inhabits our praises with love. As we enter into His gates with thanksgiving and into His courts with praise, He kisses us with His presence.

But thou art holy,
O thou that inhabits the praise of Israel.
Psalm 22:3

Praise is a form of ministry unto the Lord. It is the breath by which we express our joy and gratitude for the free gift of salvation, for who He is as the Lord of lords and King of kings, and for who we are in Him.

...I am the Alpha and the Omega,
the Beginning and the End.
I will give of the fountain of the water of life
freely to him who thirsts.
He who overcomes shall inherit all things,
and I will be his God and he shall be My son.
Revelation 21:6,7

Chapter 3
Pure in His Presence

As we delight in the Lord, let us come into His presence with a holy reverence for He is a Holy God.

Let us come with integrity and a clean heart. The Lord is not looking for perfection, but purity.

A lifestyle of thanksgiving in our hearts and praise upon our lips will cultivate a life of reverence and devotion; of integrity, inner strength and obedience to our Lord.

> *Let integrity and uprightness preserve me,*
> *For I wait for You.*
> Psalm 25:21

> *Create in me a clean heart, O God;*
> *and renew a right spirit within me.*
> Psalm 51:10

> *Search me, O God, and know my heart;*
> *test me and know my anxious thoughts.*
> *See if there is any offensive way in me,*
> *and lead me in the way everlasting.*
> Psalm 139:23,24

> *If we confess our sins,*
> *He is faithful and just to forgive us our sins*
> *and to cleanse us from all unrighteousness.*
> 1 John 1:9,10

Chapter 4

Enter into His Courts with Praise

O LORD, our Lord, how majestic is Your name in all the earth! You have set Your glory above the heavens.

Psalm 8:1

I will praise You, O LORD, with all my heart; I will tell of all Your wonders. I will be glad and rejoice in You; I will sing praise to Your name, O Most High. Psalm 9:1,2

Great is the LORD, and greatly to be praised in the city of our God, in the mountain of His holiness. Beautiful for situation, the joy of the whole earth, is mount Zion, on the sides of the north, the city of the great King. Psalm 48:1,2

Because Your loving kindness is better than life, My lips shall praise You. Thus I will bless You while I live; I will lift up my hands in Your name. Psalm 63:3,4

I will praise the name of God with a song, and will magnify Him with thanksgiving. Psalm 69:30

Bless the Lord, O my soul. O Lord my God, thou art very great; thou art clothed with honour and majesty.

Psalm 104:1

Praise ye the Lord, O give thanks unto the Lord; for He is good; for His mercy endureth forever. Psalm 106:1

I will praise You, O LORD, among the nations; I will sing of You among the peoples. For great is Your love, higher than the heavens; Your faithfulness reaches to the skies. Be exalted, O God, above the heavens, and let Your glory be over all the earth. Psalm 108:3,5

I will praise You with my whole heart, before the gods I will sing praises to You. I will worship toward Your holy temple, and praise Your name for Your lovingkindness and Your truth; for You have magnified Your word above all Your name.   Psalm 138:1,2

I will praise You, for I am fearfully and wonderfully made; Marvelous are Your works, and that my soul knows very well.   Psalm 139:14

Praise the LORD from the heavens, praise Him in the heights above. Praise Him, all His angels, praise Him, all His heavenly hosts. Praise Him, sun and moon, praise Him, all you shining stars. Praise Him, you highest heavens and you waters above the skies.   Psalm 148:1-4

Praise God in His sanctuary; Praise Him in His mighty firmament! Praise Him for His mighty acts; Praise Him according to His excellent greatness! Praise Him with the sound of the trumpet; Praise Him with the lute and harp! Praise Him with the timbrel and dance; Praise Him with stringed instruments and flutes! Praise Him with loud cymbals; Praise Him with clashing cymbals! Let everything that has breath praise the Lord.   Psalm 150

Holy, holy, holy is the Lord God Almighty, who was, and is, and is to come.   Revelation 4:8

You are worthy, O Lord, to receive glory and honor and power; for You created all things, and by Your will they exist and were created.   Revelation 4:11

...Blessing and honor and glory and power, be to Him who sits on the throne, and to the Lamb, forever and ever!
Revelation 5:13

Chapter 5
Boldly Proclaim Faith's Confessions

My life belongs to the Lord and I love Him with all my heart, with all my soul and with all my strength.
(Ref. Deuteronomy 6:5)

I delight in the Lord giving thanks in every situation and He gives me the desires of my heart.   (Ref. Psalm 37:4)

I walk in divine protection because I dwell in the secret place of the Most High. The Lord gives His angels charge over me to accompany, defend and preserve me in all my ways and no weapon formed against me will prosper.
(Ref. Psalm 91:1,2, 11; Isaiah 54:17)

I know the voice of the Lord and the voice of a stranger I do not follow, therefore I will not fall nor fail.
(Ref. John 10:4,5)

The Spirit of Truth lives in me and guides me. Therefore I have wisdom in every situation I encounter today.
(Ref. John 16:13; Romans 8:11)

I walk in love at all times because the love of God is in my heart. I am patient and kind, not touchy nor jealous nor quick to anger.   (Ref. Romans 5:5; 1 Corinthians 13:4-7)

I am free from all condemnation; for the Spirit of life in Christ Jesus has set me free from the law of sin and death.
(Ref. Roman 8:1,2)

I am a child of God, a joint heir and co-laborer with Christ Jesus and I delight to do His will.
(Ref. Romans 8:16,17; Psalm 40:8)

I'm a new person in Christ Jesus. I've been redeemed. My past has been forgiven and forgotten.
(Ref. 2 Corinthians 5:17; Psalm 103:12; Isaiah 43:25)

I am the righteousness of God through Christ Jesus; therefore, I stand in the presence of God without the sense of shame, guilt, condemnation or inferiority.
(Ref. 2 Corinthians 5:21)

I can do all things through Christ who strengthens me because greater is He that is in me than he that is in the world. (Ref. Philippians 4:13; 1 John 4:4)

I am filled with the knowledge of God's will with all wisdom and spiritual understanding.
(Ref. Colossians 1:9)

The peace of God rules my heart and I refuse to worry. The Word of God dwells in me richly and feeds my spirit on truth. (Ref. Colossians 3:15,16; Philippians 4:6)

I have a sound mind, therefore fear, confusion and lack of memory are far from me. (Ref. 2 Timothy 1:7)

I am a doer of the Word. I apply the shield of faith and the sword of the Spirit pushing back the darkness and fiery darts of evil. (Ref. James 1:22; Ephesians 6:16)

The Lord hears my prayers because I am righteous. I am blessed with all spiritual blessings and seated in heavenly places. (Ref. 1 Peter 3:12; Ephesians 1:3, 2:6)

The Lord has given me authority to trample on serpents and scorpions, and over all the power of the enemy. In the name of Jesus, I take my authority and nothing shall by any means hurt me. (Ref. Luke 10:19)

Chapter 6

An Ambassador for Christ

The Spirit of the Lord is upon me and has anointed me to preach the Gospel. He has given me the heathen as my inheritance. (Ref. Luke 4:18; Psalm 2:8)

The Lord surrounds me with favor. Therefore I walk in the overflowing favor of God and have favor with people in positions of authority and those who make decisions.
(Ref. Psalm 5:12; Proverbs 3:4)

I allow integrity and uprightness to guide me.
(Ref. Psalm 25:21)

My steps are ordered of the Lord. Therefore I have divine connections, divine appointments and supernatural relationships. (Ref. Psalm 37:23)

I have great peace because I love God's Word, taking no offense and giving no place to discouragement.
(Ref. Psalm 119:165; Deuteronomy 31:6)

I trust in the Lord with all my heart and do not lean on my own understanding. (Ref. Proverbs 3:5)

God makes a way where there seems to be no way and He supplies all my needs. (Ref. Isaiah 43:19; Philippians 4:19)

I seek first the Kingdom of God and His righteousness keeping my priorities in right order. (Ref. Matthew 6:33)

I walk in love and let no corrupt communication or gossip come out of my mouth. (Ref. John 15:12; Ephesians 4:29)

Signs and wonders follow me as I preach the Word. In the name of Jesus I speak in new tongues, I cast out demons, I lay hands on the sick and they recover.
(Ref. Mark 16:15-17; James 5:14,15)

I am not ashamed of the Gospel, for I am the salt of the earth and have been given the ministry of reconciliation.
(Ref. Romans 1:16; Matthew 5:13; 2 Corinthians 5:18)

The eyes of my understanding are enlightened to His calling. I know His will for my life and I walk in it with clarity of vision, confidence and an inner knowing.
(Ref. Ephesians 1:18; 1 John 2:20)

I am strengthened with might by God's Spirit in my inner man. I am rooted and grounded in His love; therefore, I walk by faith and not by sight.
(Ref. Ephesians 3:16-20; 2 Corinthians 5:7)

Utterance is given unto me and I boldly proclaim the Gospel as an Ambassador for Jesus Christ. (Ref. Ephesians 6:19)

I will not be defeated because the Lord has begun a good work in me and He shall complete it. (Ref. Philippians 1:6)

I will keep my faith and a good conscience. I will fight a good fight and finish my course.
(Ref. 1 Timothy 1:19; 2 Timothy 4:7)

I reflect the nature of Jesus in my attitude, conversation and lifestyle. (Ref. 1 Timothy 4:12)

I humble myself before the Lord that I might decrease and He might increase. (Ref. 1 Peter 5:6; John 3:30)

Chapter 7
Financial Blessings

It is the Lord who gives me power to get wealth to establish His covenant. (Ref. Deuteronomy 8:18)

I'm blessed coming in and blessed going out, I'm above and not beneath, I'm the head and not the tail. I am the lender and not the borrower. (Ref. Deuteronomy 28:3-13)

I meditate on the Word of God daily and my pathway is prosperous and successful. (Ref. Joshua 1:8)

I shout for joy and magnify the Lord who takes pleasure in my prosperity. (Ref. Psalm 35:27)

I give to the poor, therefore I have no lack. (Ref. Proverbs 28:27)

I bring my tithes into the storehouse and the windows of heaven are opened unto me. The Lord pours out His blessings upon me. I proclaim my bank accounts and investments are blessed of the Lord. (Ref. Malachi 3:10)

I am a giver, therefore it is given unto me, good measure, pressed down, shaken together and running over, shall men give unto me. (Ref. Luke 6:38)

The Lord causes every blessing to come to me so that in all circumstances and whatever my need, I am self-sufficient, possessing enough to require no aid or support and furnished in abundance for every good work and charitable donation. (Ref. 2 Corinthians 9:8)

Chapter 8

Victory for Family, Leaders and Nations

It is written: If I believe on the Lord Jesus Christ, I shall be saved and my house. Therefore, I claim salvation for _____ in Jesus name. (Ref. Acts 16:31)

_____*'s head is anointed with oil and his/her burden is lifted and the yoke is destroyed because of the anointing.* (Ref. Psalm 23:5; Isaiah 10:27)

_____ *has been trained in the ways of the Lord and shall not depart from it.* (Ref. Proverbs 22:6)

_____ *is a disciple taught of the Lord and great is his/her peace and undisturbed composure.* (Ref. Isaiah 54:13)

_____ *is free from the land of the enemy (drug abuse, alcohol, homosexuality) and comes back to his/her own borders.* (Ref. Jeremiah 31:16,17)

_____ *hungers and thirsts after righteousness and follows the voice of the Lord.* (Ref. Matthew 5:6)

_____ *is free from deception, demonic strongholds and spiritual blindness because truth has set him/her free. And whom the Son sets free is free indeed.* (Ref. John 8:32)

_____ *is filled with the knowledge of God's will with all wisdom and spiritual understanding.* (Ref. Colossians 1:9)

_____ *loves the Lord with all his/her heart, soul and mind.* (Ref. Deuteronomy 6:5)

Chapter 9

God's Medicine for Healing and Staying Healthy

It is written: I am healed from all diseases and my life has been delivered from all destruction. (Ref. Psalm 103:3,4)

It is written: I shall not die but live and declare the works of the Lord for I am satisfied with long life and I walk in divine health. (Ref. Psalm 118:17; Psalm 91:16)

It is written: By His stripes I am healed. (Ref. Isaiah 53:4,5; 1 Peter 2:24)

It is written: No weapon formed against me shall prosper. (Ref. Isaiah 54:17)

It is written: I am strong, and My health is restored speedily. (Ref. Joel 3:10; Isaiah 58:8)

It is written: Himself bore my sickness and carried my diseases so that I do not have to carry them. (Ref. Matthew 8:17)

It is written: Resist the devil and he will flee. Satan, I give you NO place. I take authority over you and pull you down from your position of authority breaking the power of assignment you have against me. Now flee in Jesus name. (Ref. Ephesians 4:27; Luke 10:19; James 4:7)

It is written: I discipline my body. Therefore I purpose to put my flesh under. I resist the temptation of eating junk food and of over eating. (Ref. 1 Corinthians 9:27)

(for women) *It is written: I shall not suffer miscarriage or be barren.* (Ref. Exodus 23:26)

Chapter 10

Our Covenant Keeping God

When we become a Christian through the new birth, we enter into a covenant with God. Our covenant-God will love us forever and will always be with us.

Therefore know that the LORD your God, He is God, the faithful God who keeps covenant and mercy for a thousand generations with those who love Him and keep His commandments. Deuteronomy 7:9

...I will never leave you nor forsake you. Hebrews 13:5

When we proclaim God's Word, He is always ready to bring it to pass. It will never return void.

... for I will hasten my word to perform it. Jeremiah 1:12

... It shall not return to Me void, but it shall accomplish what I please, and it shall prosper in the thing for which I sent it. Isaiah 55:11

What God has said in His Word is forever settled in Heaven. It cannot and will not be changed. He is faithful forever. Through His Word He causes us to triumph.

Thanks be to God who always leads us in triumph in Christ... 2 Corinthians 2:14

...Blessing and honor and glory and power, be to Him who sits on the throne, and to the Lamb, forever and ever! Revelation 5:13

25

Personal Thoughts, Prayers and Victories

Personal Thoughts, Prayers and Victories

To order product contact:

Marilyn Neubauer Ministries
P.O. Box 4664
Oceanside, CA 92052

(760) 439-1401
www.marilynneubauer.com

Other books by Dr. Marilyn Neubauer:

Welcome to the Family
Book and workbook

(A guide for new believers
and also an excellent tool for cell groups
as a refreshing of the basics
for our Christian walk.)

Instruction from the Great Physician

(God's instructions regarding His Word
are health [medicine] to our flesh [Proverbs 4:22].
His medicine has no negative side effects and will
bring healing to our physical bodies.)

All are available in German and Spanish.
To order products in the German translation, please contact:

Zoe Gospel Center
Badenerstrasse 808
CH-8048 Zürich / Switzerland
Tel. +41 44 432 9272

Triumphant Living
Marilyn Neubauer Ministries

Dr. Marilyn Neubauer was born and raised in Nebraska and gave her heart to the Lord as a young child.

She has served in ministry since 1977. Marilyn ministers throughout the United States and abroad doing extensive missions work, teaching in Bible Schools, conferences and churches, emphasizing God's love, divine healing, and His deep desire for an intimate relationship with His children.

Marilyn's teaching focuses primarily on the Biblical truths about healing. Her personal testimonies of healing from cancer, the miraculous disappearance of a tumor, and her near-death experience with malaria bring hope and encouragement to the Body of Christ.

Marilyn lives in San Diego, California and serves her community as an active Chaplain for the Oceanside Police Department.

Marilyn has received a Doctor of Divinity degree from Cambridge Theological Seminary.

Made in the USA
San Bernardino, CA
07 April 2015